An Introduction to
Playing Blues and Ballads on the Piano
by
Dr Jazz

Book1: The essential elements

Clinical Press

© *Paul R Goddard,* **2024**

The right of Paul R Goddard to be identified as the author and artist of this work has been asserted by him in accordance with the Copyright, Designs and Patents Act 1988.

All rights reserved. No part of this publication may be reproduced, stored in a retrieval system, or transmitted in any form or by any means, electronic, mechanical, photocopying, recording or otherwise, without prior permission from the copyright owner.

While the advice and information in this book is believed to be true and accurate at the time of going to press, neither the author, the editor, nor the publisher can accept legal responsibility for any errors or omissions that may be made. The publisher makes no warranty, express or implied, with respect to the material contained herein.

First published in the UK 2024

Published by:

Clinical Press Ltd. Redland Green Farm, Redland, Bristol, BS6 7HF

A catalogue record for this book is available from the British Library

ISBN 978-1-85457-120-5

An Introduction to Playing Blues and Ballads on the Piano. Book 1: The essential elements by Dr Jazz   published by Clinical Press Ltd. 2024

Also available from Clinical Press:

ISBN 978-1-85457-125-0 *An Introduction To Playing the Blues on the Dr. Jazz Slide Guitar* Clinical Press Ltd. 2023

ISBN: 978-1-85457-122-9 *Make your own slide guitar*

ISBN 978-1-85457-0925 *Arthur's Favourite Hymns and Thoughts for the Day* Goddard A.F., Goddard P.R.

Songs in this book

Title	Page Number
The Blues Will Drive Me Mad	10
Midnight With the Blues	12-13
Down in the Valley	16
Frankie and Johnnie	20-21
CC Rider	22
Blues in G (Blue Pyjama Blues)	24
Forget-Me-Nots	26-27
I Ain't Got Nobody	28
Streets of Laredo (The Cowboy's Lament)	30

Chapter 1

The Blues are great fun to play and easy to learn. In this book I will show you how to cheat and play basic piano tunes, in particular those with the feel of the blues.

Improvisation is a form of composition based on the structure of an already existing piece of music. With other members of the band also improvising at the same time the music will have a unique and spontaneous nature peculiar to blues and jazz.

Instrumental music is made up of three main elements

- Melody
- Harmony
- Rhythm

Add to that the vocals and you've got the lot!

Since the piano is an instrument that encompasses all the basic aspects of music, for a pianist to improvise he has to have some understanding of all three. But it is not difficult! Do not despair!

All of the pieces have been videoed and put on Youtube. Although roughly following the score, in the spirit of the blues the recordings do not keep strictly to the written music. This is intentional and gives a simple indication of the way in which the music can be spontaneously interpreted. In particular note that the pieces are often played with an element of swing that is difficult to encompass in the written score.

Playing without written music:
Is it possible to learn to play the blues without being able to read music?

These books have been designed for both the would-be pianist who cannot read music and for the competent pianist. Some people are so gifted that they can simply listen and play. Such people can often already compose and improvise and are therefore unlikely to be reading these tutorials.

Rather than aiming at the unbridled genius who can do it all already, we shall address the pianist who is competent at playing from written music but wishes to learn to 'play by ear' and to improvise and compose **and** the person with a good ear but no knowledge of written music.

It is undoubtedly true that it would be easier for the students if they at least learn to pick out the melody lines from the musical score treble clef. This is not, however, essential since the tutorials are accompanied by recordings of all of the musical pieces available on YouTube and many of the tunes have also been written out as melody lines using a simple lettering scheme.

A pianist will find it very hard to compose if he or she plays exclusively from written scores. 'Following the tadpoles' does permit one to play a huge variety of already composed music and can inform the player. However it does not stimulate the compositional talents.

To get away from the written score the player must learn to play by ear. For most people it is essential to learn some of the basic harmonic and melodic theory first, in order that what they hear can be understood.

Whenever we learn a new skill there must be an element of effort put in by the pupil but this does not need to be excessive.

So how can I discard the music when I cannot even remember how to play simple pieces?

Don't learn the pieces by rote in the manner of a classical concert pianist. These tutorials will **not** require the willing victim to put in hours of practice a day. 30 minutes practice a day should more than suffice and it is hoped that the pupil will find the challenge so enjoyable that they find themselves performing rather than practising. As the pupil learns to improvise they will gradually realise that it is not difficult to learn to play and improvise in public. In fact most of the performers you see on television hammering away at pianos and often singing too, find it simple for one single reason. They are only performing simple stuff! Once you understand the structure of the music this much becomes apparent.

Goddard Golden Rule number one
Only play your easy pieces in public

Most of the public cannot appreciate which music is easy and which is hard. There is no point trying to impress an audience by playing pieces you cannot complete or keep in time. So stick to the easy stuff!

Don't despise simple music. It is often the most soulful. It can be the hardest to compose… to create an original but simple piece of music is difficult since much has already been done.

Chapter 2

What is the keyboard and how does it relate to the written score?

A part of

The Keyboard

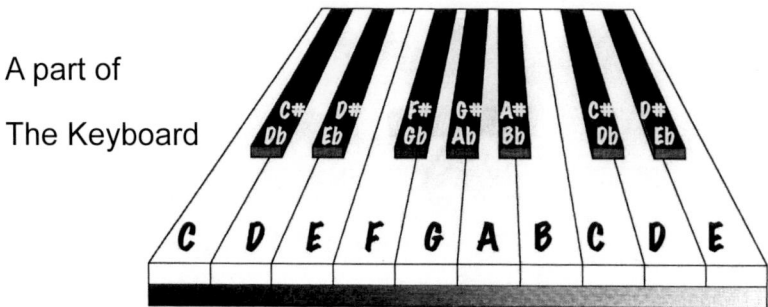

I'm sure you have noticed that there are black and white notes. The pitch ascends from the left to the right with a semitone difference between each adjacent note including black and white keys. Now observe that the black notes are grouped alternately in a pair and a triplet. The note C is to be found immediately to the left of a pair of black notes. On a normal piano Middle C is to be found almost exactly in the middle of the keyboard (situated to the left of a pair of black notes as usual).

If we start with C we can ascend the keyboard in semitones by moving to the right. We would immediately hit a black note between the C and the D. This can either be known as C sharp(C#) or D flat (Db) since the note is one and the same.

The sharp has the symbol # and refers to the raising of a note by a semitone. The flat has the symbol ♭ (which looks like a b)and refers to the lowering of a note by a semitone.

The next note is **D**, the next **D# (Eb)** and so on as follows

E, F,F# (Gb), G, G# (Ab), A , A# (Bb), B

and back to C (one octave higher than at the start).

If we want to play a simple major scale of C we miss out the black notes.

Up   CDEFGABC

Down CBAGFEDC

This can been notated as on the score below:

In the treble clef

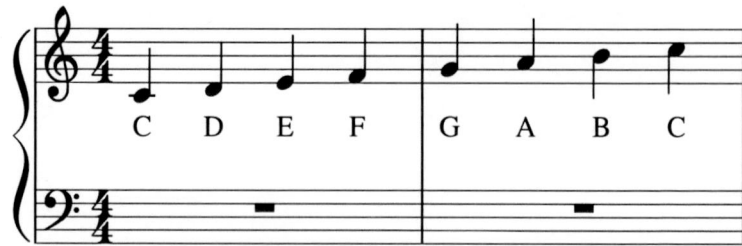

And in the bass clef

Treble clef and bass clef can be considered as a continuous set of 11 lines with the middle line being the line through the middle C …..to make reading of the score easier the line is invisible unless there is a note on it, middle C, or projecting below it from above, B, or above it from below, D.

But what is the structure of the music?

We will start with harmony.

Western music uses harmony based on the 'Tempered scale'. This we know and sing as do, re, me, far etc.

This method of tuning was proposed as early as 1482 and particularly applies to keyboard instruments. Bach famously wrote pieces for 'the well-tempered clavier'.

Each note is tuned so that it is proportionately the same number of vibrations apart from the next. This is a practical mathematical compromise so that chords played in different keys can still be in harmony with a melody and in order that modulation through the keys is possible.

One early composer, Jean-Phillippe Rameau, announced in 1726 that *'Melody stems from harmony'*. In Western music, if the harmony is complex, this is frequently the case.

Chords

If notes are the elements of music then chords are the molecules of harmony. Chords are a collection of three or more different notes struck together at the same time (or played so that they are effectively overlapping).

The more simple the harmony, the simpler the chords used. Thus a simple nursery rhyme, a rudimentary hymn or a patriotic march may be harmonised by major chords based on the major triad. For the key of C the major triad would be the notes C, E and G.

A more complex piece of music will often involve the use of a number of different chords often using minor keys and sevenths.

The most commonly used chords in the key of C will be shown here. These do have to be learnt and memorised at some stage for the pupil to be able to compose or improvise with ease but at the moment they have been included here for completeness and in order that later parts of the text can be understood.

The Chords of C

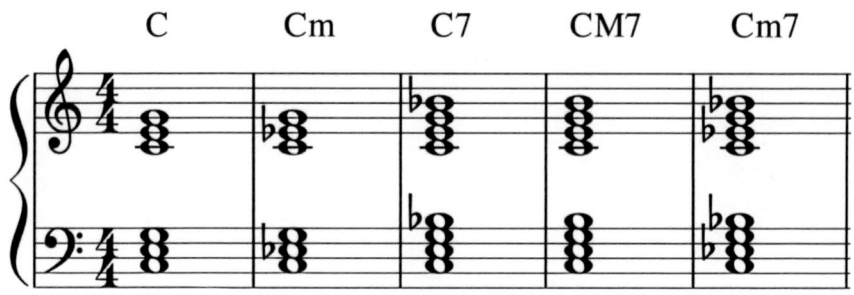

Chord name

C major   C minor   C seventh   C major seventh   C minor seventh

Notes of the chord (both hands

C E G   C Eb G   C E G Bb   C E G B   C Eb G Bb

At this stage first try to learn the chords C major, minor and seven. Other chords can come later.

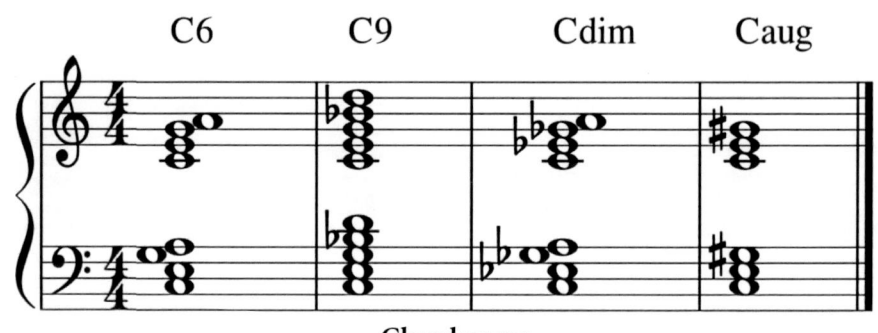

Chord name

C six   C nine   C diminished   C augmented

Notes of the chord (both hands

C E G A   C E G Bb D   C Eb Gb A   C E G#

These are examples of the chords in C. They can be repeated in all the other keys by working out the intervals between the notes.

In addition they can be played in a different spatial order creating inversions which help the flow and feel of the music. Here are the three most important chords shown on the keyboard to help the novice players.

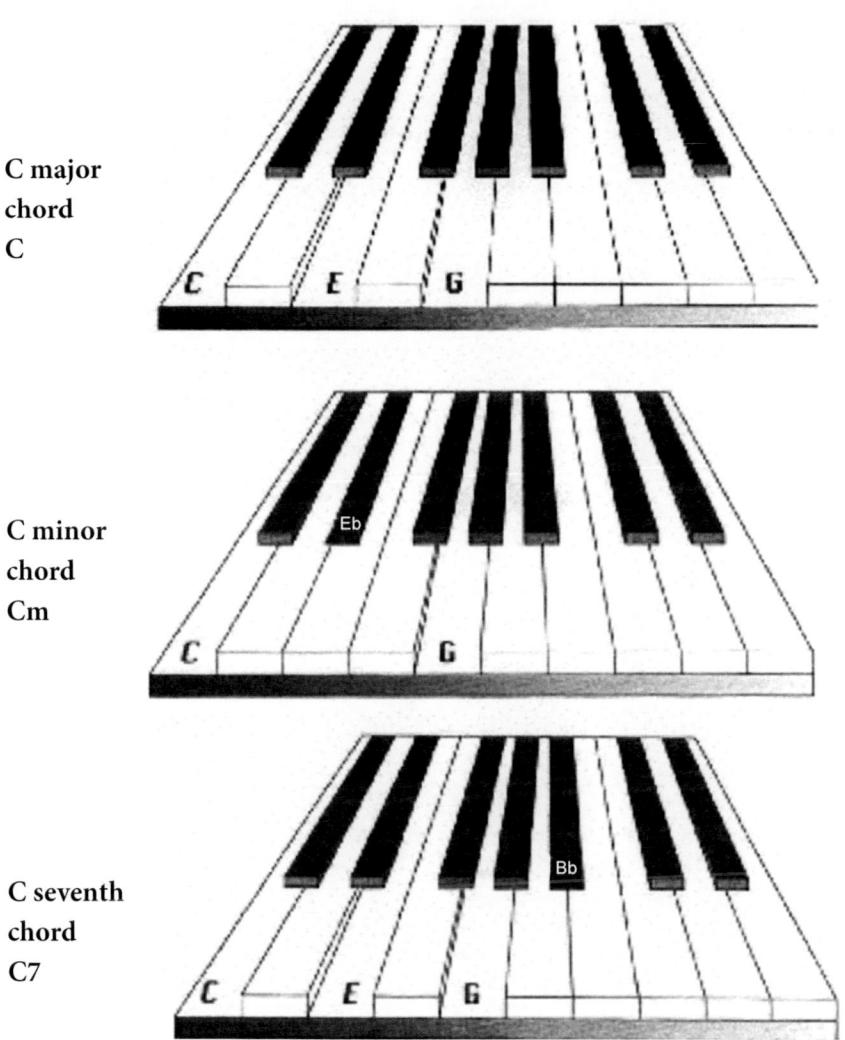

C major
chord
C

C minor
chord
Cm

C seventh
chord
C7

Try these out with both hands until you understand where they are. On future pages they will be simply referred to as C, Cm and C7.

Let's start playing the blues.. *The Blues Will Drive Me Mad*

A simple 12 bar blues is scored below with the melody written in lower case letters below the chord letter. Above the score are the guitar chords which are also the chords you should play on the piano to accompany this blues. If you cannot play the chords yet just play the single note in the bass or try arpeggios (where the notes of the chord are sounded individually). https://bit.ly/BluesDriveMeMad. This is followed by a harder piece for the experienced pianist to play and examine its structure. https://bit.ly/MidnightWithTheBlues for *Midnight With The Blues*.

Chords used in *Blues will drive me mad*

This piece can be harmonised using the chords written above the score. The C chords **C** and **C7** were shown on pages 5 and 6 of this tutorial.

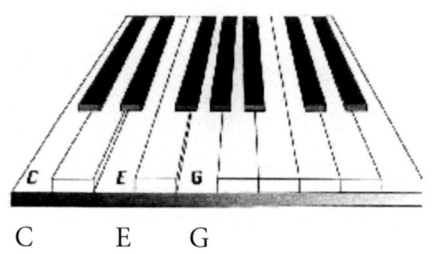

C major   C   E   G

The Chord of F7   F   A   C   Eb

For F9 a G is added at the top but this is found in the melody line

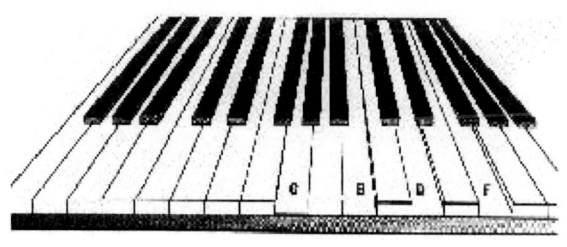

The Chord of G7   G   B   D   F

For G9 the note A is added at the top. Once again this is found in the melody line. Next, a full score of a piece written for the more expert player.

Midnight With The Blues

P Goddard

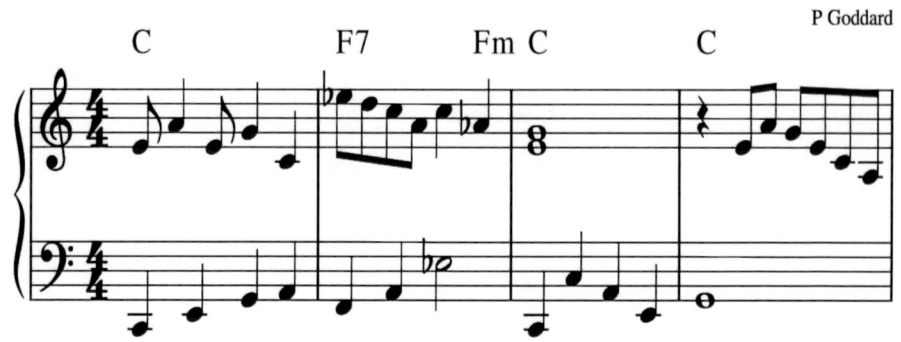

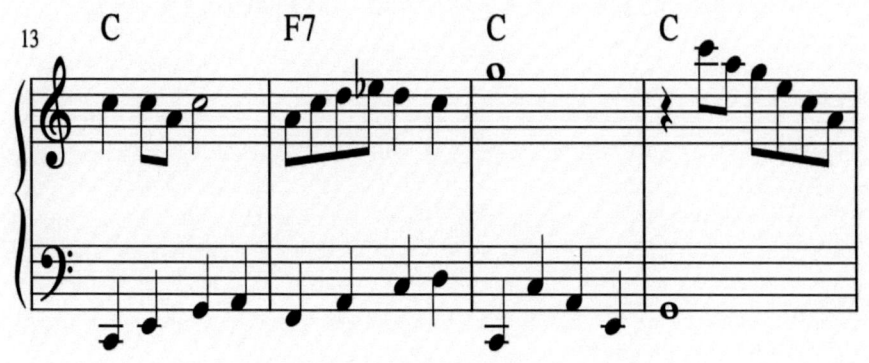
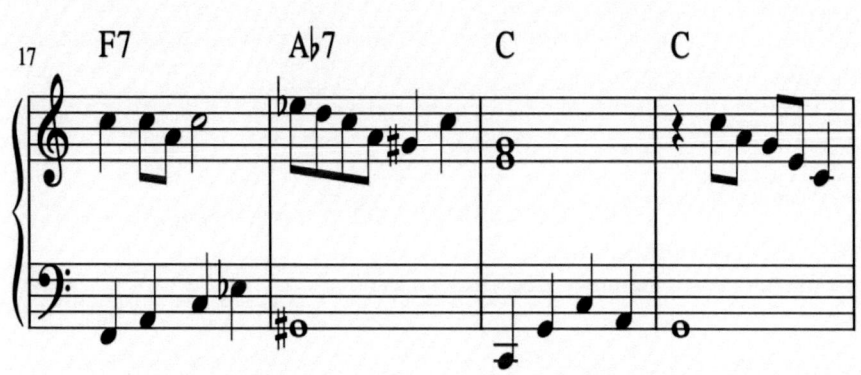

Chapter 3 Chord Sequences

How do I choose a chord sequence and why does one chord naturally lead to another? The answer is Chord Sequences.

Just like the use of the tempered scale the use of harmonic chord sequences is a conditioned or learnt response. Other systems of music may use fewer notes (for example the pentatonic scale as used in West Africa) or may use many more notes (as in the quarter-tones used in India). The harmonies based on these scales sound correct to a person brought up in the local tradition.

However, having once accepted the 'tempered tuning' (as on the piano) the harmonic modulations in Western music follow a very logical progression.

There are three simple rules governing progression of chords that I use when composing and improvising. My analysis shows that most popular Western music uses one or more of these rules. The use of even just these three rules provides an almost infinite variety of harmonic progressions or chord sequences.

The rules are:

1. *The Cycle of Keys*, 2. *Descent in semitones*, and 3. *Substitute chords*

This chapter will concentrate on the first of these, the cycle of keys, and its importance in the blues.

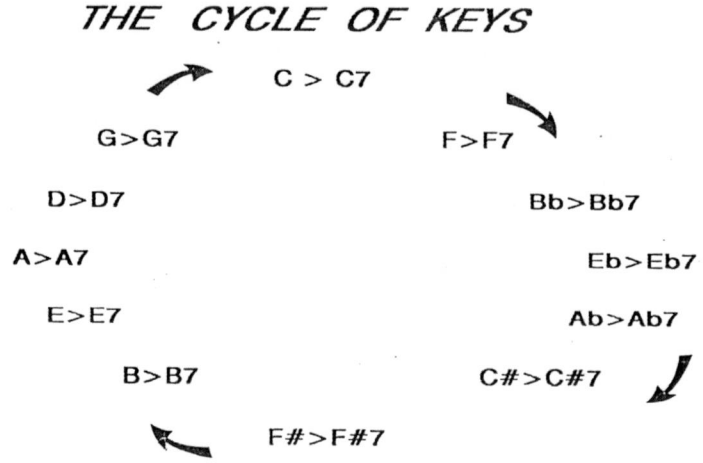

I have drawn the cycle of keys as progressing in a clockwise direction from the first chord to the fourth. Thus starting from C the progression is to F and on to Bb etc. Sometimes the cycle of keys is drawn the opposite way round (anti-clockwise) but to my mind the natural progression is as shown. The cycle can also be described as moving from the fifth to the first since C is the fifth note of the F major scale.

Although still perfectly acceptable it is harder to move in the opposite direction. So G to C is easy and can be likened to going down hill. Going from C to G is like going uphill and creates the desire in the music for the harmony to return to the original point i.e. the chord of C.

So we immediately have a way of creating a harmonic progression in a piece of music by using the cycle of keys. This progression can be thought of as being similar to a journey. If we call C our original tonal area we could go on a little journey uphill to the tonal area of G then toddle back down again to C. A piece of music can be written with only two chords and on the next page is a very beautiful example: *Down in the Valley*.

The two chords are G and D. You start in G , move to D then back to G, alternating between the chords and eventually ending in G.

The song is a traditional American folk song and its alternative title is *Birmingham Jail*. It is in ¾ time: three beats to the bar which is also known as waltz time (think: oom pah pah).

When you play this piece from the score you must take note of the key signature. The song is written in the key of G and that means that the f# (f-sharp) sign is at the beginning of both staves. Whenever you meet the f in the score it must be played as a sharpened note (a semi-tone up).

Practice this piece making up the chords for the left hand. In order to emphasise the beat they can be played as arpeggios or as I have scored them, an oom pah pah line (1,5,5)! You do not have to keep to this! In a later chapter we will look at other bass lines.

Having learnt to sing the tune or hum it to ourselves we should put the music away and play this from memory and get ready to play it to a friend.

Here is *Down in the Valley* on video:

https://bit.ly/DownValley

Goddard Golden Rule number two
When performing, if you make a mistake, don't stop.

Careful research compared amateur and professional musicians playing from musical scores. The research used eye-tracking devices and the

Down In The Valley

researchers expected to find that professionals read further ahead in the music. This was not the case. The one significant difference was that when the professionals made a mistake they did not stop. They ignored it and carried on. Do the same when you are playing from ear or from memory. Just keep going and make sure to finish on the right chord and it will usually sound OK.

Down in the valley, the valley so low
Hang your head over, hear the wind blow
Hear the wind blow dear, hear the wind blow
Hang your head over, hear the wind blow.

Roses love sunshine, violets love dew
Angels in heaven know I love you
Know I love you dear, know I love you
Angels in heaven know I love you.

If you don't love me, love whom you please
Throw your arms round me, give my heart ease
Give my heart ease love, give my heart ease
Throw your arms round me give my heart ease.

Build me a castle forty feet high
So I can see her as she rides by
As she rides by love as she rides by
So I can see her as she rides by.

Write me a letter send it by mail
Send it in care of Birmingham jail
Birmingham jail love, Birmingham jail
Send it in care of Birmingham jail.

Homework from chapter 3

1) Analyse some of your sheet music at home and see whether any of it follows the cycle of keys at any point. It's bound to!

2) Practise *Down in the Valley* until you can play it from memory and then start playing different notes from the same chords in the right hand and playing arpeggios. This is one way to start improvising. Write the chords out as a chord chart and keep them in a little hard back book or a loose leaf file. Note the time signature at the beginning of each chord chart.

Chapter 4.
The Origin of the Blues

The Blues and Jazz developed where West African music, with its pentatonic scale and complex rhythms, met European music (with its 'tempered' harmonies and 4/4 and 3/4 beats). Hymns and marches greatly influenced early ragtime and jazz and Roman Catholic musical traditions influenced Latin American music but the improvisational and rhythmic element was mainly African.

Melody

The plaintive melodies of the blues have developed because of the clash between the pentatonic natural scales of the Africans and the mathematical 'well-tempered' scale of the Europeans. Particularly important notes are the third and the seventh. The natural note for a 3rd lies somewhere between the flattened (minor) 3rd and the major 3rd. Thus the natural 3rd in the key of C would lie between Eb and E. The blues singer will slide the note over this small range providing the classical blue note. The same occurs between the flattened 7th and major $7^{th.}$ The 7th note is slurred between the two in blues singing. In the key of C this would be between Bb and B.

On the piano we do not have the luxury of sliding between notes but playing two together or quickly moving from one note to another as a grace note can provide the same effect.

The blues partly developed from 'field hollers'. In these a leader would sing a line and the other workers in the field would copy it. This is the earliest version of call and response, where an individual sings a line and the audience sing a response, which may be different from the first line. There are traditions of this everywhere in the world and you can hear examples in most religious ceremonies.

The blues lyrics often repeat themselves in a call and response manner.

Rhythm and Structure of the Blues

The blues are usually played with a certain amount of syncopation. Syncopation has been jokingly likened to the actions of a drunkard.....uneven movement from bar to bar. In reality it is an emphasis of the beat by playing on the off-beat (which sounds like a paradox but works).

There are many differing chord sequences for the blues but the twelve bar blues are the most famous and are what people understand when you say " I'm going to play the blues"

The Twelve Bar Blues

Nobody knows exactly where and when the twelve bar blues developed because the music was not written down or recorded. Somewhere around 1910 the 12 bar blues started to be performed in New Orleans and neighbouring towns. It was then taken to Chicago and New York when the red-light district of New Orleans was illegally and forcibly closed down in 1918.

Some people say that *Careless Love* (written down by W C Handy) is the earliest written blues. It certainly has the blues sentiment in the lyrics and the lyrical lines are often repeated in a blues-like manner. But it is a 16 bar song not a 12 bar piece and does not qualify as the earliest 12-bar blues.

I have made a careful examination of 18th and 19th century music and twelve bar pieces are surprisingly rare. Most short songs are of 8 or 16 bars. I have found a couple of carols of 12 bars and the well-known nursery rhyme *Ding Dong Bell*. This rhyme has a 12 bar structure and a call and response form and the lyrics include a moral message (be kind to animals). The origins of this nursery rhyme date back to the 16th century. Shakespeare uses the phrase in the Tempest - Act I, Scene II:

"Sea nymphs hourly ring his knell:
Hark! Now I hear them - Ding, dong, bell".

There is a later song which still pre-dates all other written or recorded blues and is extremely famous. This is Frankie and Johnny...said to have been heard around the 1850s and according to Sandburg, already popular among railroaders of the west & along the Mississippi River by 1888. Also known as Frankie and Albert, Frankie's Blues, Sadie or Josie, the song reputedly referred to an actual event. Note that the f and the c are sharpened when playing the tune in the key of D. On the next page it is in C. This version was written down by Hughie Cannon who also penned *Won't You Come Home Bill Bailey?*

Frankie and Johnny

Chord Sequences of the Blues

The chord sequence of Frankie and Johnny as written opposite can be simplified to

```
D    /  D  /  D              /  D
G    /  G  /  G              /  D
Em   /  A9      /  D         /  D
```

This is a very simple version of the standard 12 bar blues sequence. It is based on the initial harmonic tonal area of D and the chords of G and A . As described in Tutorial 2 the A and G are immediately adjacent on the Cycle of Keys. The E minor adds a extra interest to the progression and can be thought of as an inversion of G6. You can play this in any key you like so here it is in the key of C. On the recording the song is first played in C then moves up a full tone to D.

https://bit.ly/FrankieAndJohnny

1. Frankie and John-ny were sweet-hearts   Oh what a coup-le in love   Frank-ie was loy-al to

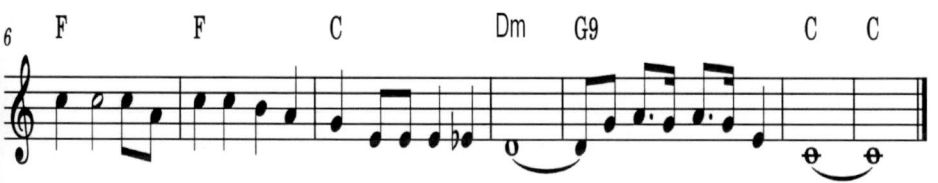

John-ny just as true as stars a - bove And he was her man   but he was do-ing her wrong

Practice Frankie and Johnny until you can remember it. Whilst singing the words or humming to yourself look only at the chords above and play the tune and harmony. Make up the melody by ear and don't worry if you get it wrong. It doesn't matter. Try it in D and in C.

Goddard Golden Rule number three

If you make a mistake when you are improvising, repeat it. The repetition of the original mistake turns it retrospectively into part of your intended improvisation.

Next we have another traditional 12 bar blues, beloved of Louis Armstrong and other early pioneers of Jazz and blues: *CC Rider. (or See See Rider)*
Here is a link to the recording:https://bit.ly/SeeSeeRider

CC Rider

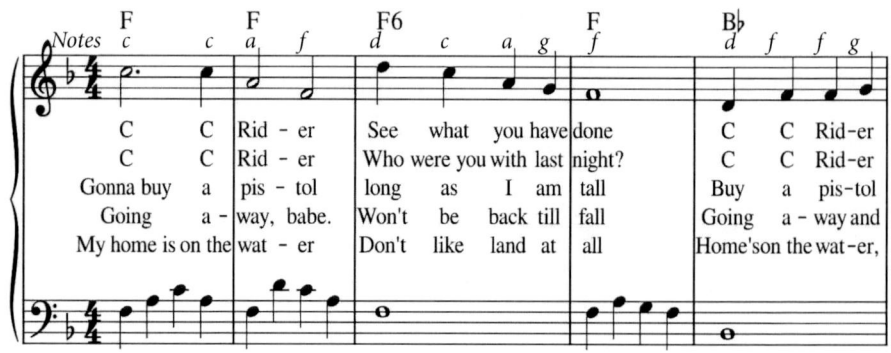

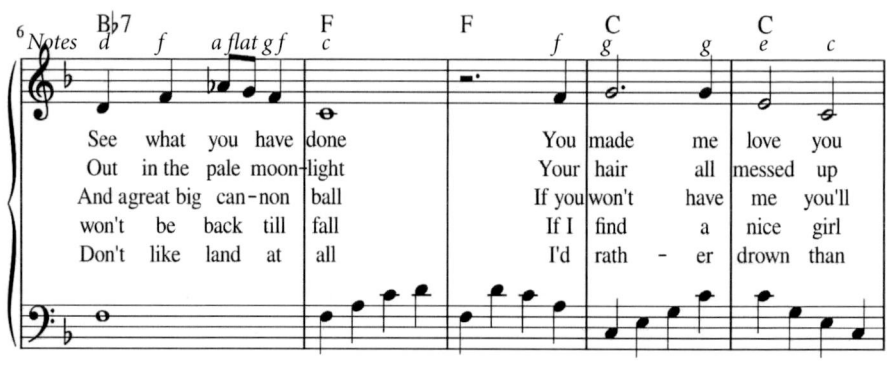

Chapter 5

In the last few pages we learnt that the music most commonly termed the blues consists of 12 bars.
In fact the number of bars in most popular music consists of a multiple of 4.
Ragtime, for example, is usually made up of a musical theme of 16 or 32 bars, each bar being 4 beats in a ragged 4/4 . There are usually 4 different themes.
Reggae is often a theme of 8 bars which is repeated (with the same words), followed by a new theme of 8 bars which is again repeated (etc.)
Ballads are often 16 bar musical themes followed by the same 16 bar theme with different words, then an 8 or 16 bar middle section (the famous middle 8), then the original 16 bar theme. This sequence can be remembered as A,A,B,A and has very commonly been used in popular music.

Blues in G

Over the page is a full piano score for a blues in the key of G. The 4 bar introductory section is included then the main 12 bar tune.
Ignoring the introduction the shape of this blues is

G / C / G / G /   C / C/ G / G /   D / C / G / G

If you use the turn round (as in the introduction) the last bar is a D
We can number the chords and make this generic. If G is taken as 1 then C is 4 and D is 5. Just sing do, re, mi and count the notes to work out why we are numbering them this way.

1 / 4 / 1 / 1 /   4 / 4 / 1 / 1 /   5 / 4 / 1 / 1

You could miss out the 4th in the second bar and replace it with the 1st.
This is probably the most common sequence for the traditional 12 bar blues. You can see by analysing Frankie and Johnny how similar this sequence is to that old ballad. If D is 1 then we have:

1/1/1/   4/4/4/ / 2minor/ 5/ 1/ 1
D/D/D/D/   G/G/G/D/   Emin / A / D /D

Variations on this sequence can of course be used in any key. Thus it is very easy to transpose the harmony of the simple 12 bar blues into any key that you may wish. Here is the standard sequence in F and it is very similar but not identical to the CC Rider sequence.

F / Bb / F / F /   Bb / Bb / F / F /   C / Bb / F / F

Blues in G (Blue Pyjama Blues)

Here is the link to the video: **https://bit.ly/3YXArow**

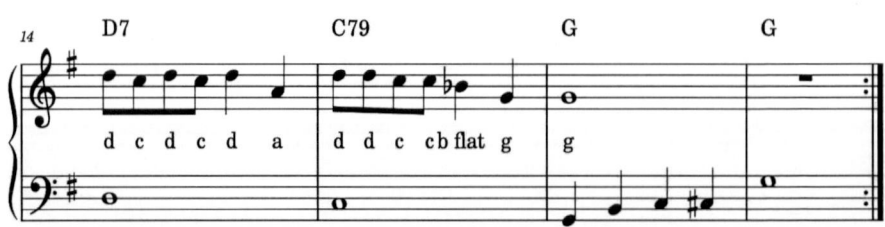

On the opposite page we have a 12 bar blues in G. This is the *Blue Pyjama Blues* and is similar to the *CC Rider*. This particular melody is a blues standard and is used in *Blue Pyjama Blues, Give Me a T for Texas, We're Going to Move to the Outskirts of Town* and many other blues.

Improvising melodies in the blues

That's covered the harmonic progression of the standard blues and given a few examples of the melody. I expect you have noticed in this last example that the b-flat note has been used extensively in the melody. In the key of G this is the flattened third (count up do, re, mi and flatten the mi!).

Another important blue note is the flattened seventh, (flattened ti) and in the key of G this is the f-natural.

Improvisation in the blues often uses pentatonic (5 note) scales.

For example in the key of C the descending scale c, b-flat, g, f, e-flat, then down to a c the octave lower.

Playing around with the blues scales can create blues runs up and down the keyboard but when you are improvising on a particular blues it is important to use some of the actual melody in your improvisation to keep the audience onboard!

Goddard Golden Rule Number 4
When you are improvising; embrace the chaos. Let your hands fall wherever they like then pull the melodies and harmonies back towards those of the original tune. Don't forget to finish on the correct chord and it will sound OK.

Chapter 6. Descent and ascent in Semitones

Forget-Me-Nots (link:https://bit.ly/4g9zgZk)

P Goddard P Goddard

Descent and ascent in Semitones

We have mainly concerned ourselves with the cycle of keys and the 12 bar blues. Also useful is descent in semitones. This can be worked into a 12 bar blues as in the example on this page. "But there are 16 bars," I hear you say! Yes, but the last 4 bars have been repeated and that is where the descent in semitones is to be found, particularly in the bass. Next we shall play a song from 1915: *I Ain't Got Nobody*. The descent in semitones is even more obvious than in *Forget-Me-Nots*. If you need to do so write the melody in your little book of songs as letters.

I Ain't Got Nobody

Graham and Williams

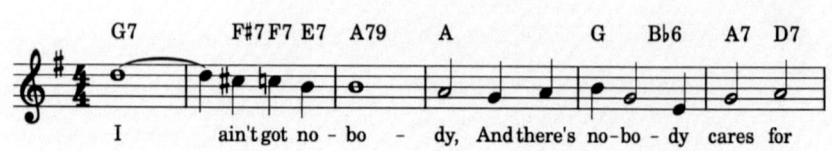
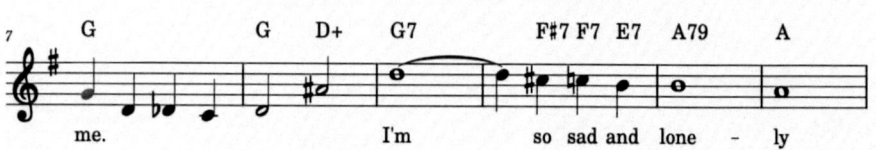
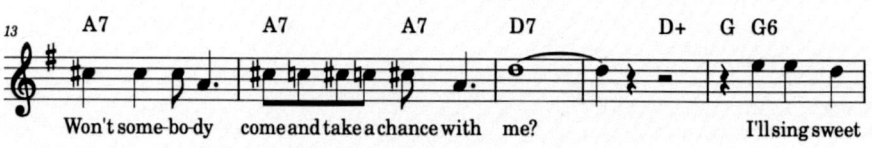
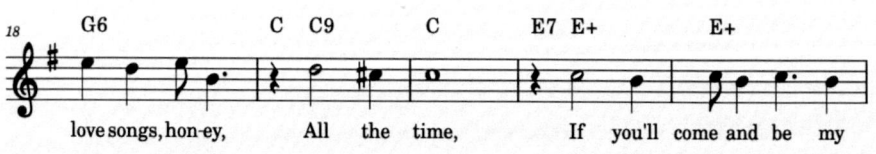

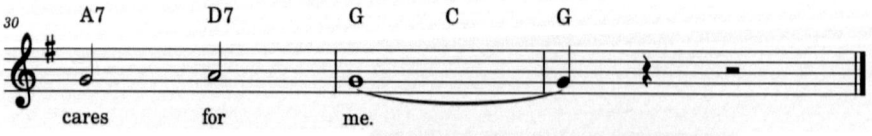

And the link is here: https://bit.ly/4dTLJ1e

Chapter 7

Bard of Armagh and The Streets of Laredo

Link:https://bit.ly/3SZ8lW0

When William of Orange was busy pushing the Protestant agenda in Ireland the Roman Catholic Bishop of Armagh went into hiding as a bard. Here we have some more detail from Wikipedia:

"The Bard of Armagh" Songwriter(s)   Patrick Donnelly

"The Bard of Armagh" is an Irish ballad. It is often attributed to Patrick Donnelly. He was made Bishop of Dromore in 1697, the same year as the enactment of the 1697 Banishment Act which was intended to clear out all Roman Catholic clergy from Ireland. Donnelly is believed to have taken the pseudonym and disguise of the travelling harper Phelim Brady.

Oh list to the lay of a poor Irish harper,
And scorn not the strings in his old withered hands,
But remember those fingers, they once could move sharper,
To raise up the strains of his dear native land.

When I was a young lad, King Jamie did flourish
And I followed the wars in my brogues bound with straw
And all the fair colleens from Wexford to Durrish
Called me bold Phelim Brady, the Bard of Armagh.

It was long before the shamrock, the dear isle's loved emblem,
Was crushed in its beauty by the Saxon lion's paw,
I was called by the colleens around me assembling
Their bold Phelim Brady, the Bard of Armagh.

How I love to muse on the days of my boyhood,
Though four score and three years have flitted since then.
Still it gives sweet reflection, as every first joy should,
For free-hearted boys make the best of old men.

At the fair or the wake I could twirl my shillelagh,
Or trip through a jig with my brogues bound with straw.
Faith, all the pretty girls in the village and the valley
Loved bold Phelim Brady, the Bard of Armagh.

Now though I have wandered this wide world over,
Still Ireland's my home and a parent to me.
Then O, let the turf that my bosom shall cover
Be cut from the ground that is trod by the free.

And when in his cold arms Death shall embrace me,
Och! lull me asleep with sweet 'Erin-go-Bragh',
By the side of my Kathleen, my first love, then place me,
Then forget Phelim Brady, the Bard of Armagh.

To the same tune and with a similar theme (dying, death and burial) we now have the **Streets of Laredo (The Cowboy's Lament).** This was written by a cowboy, Frank Maynard, in 1879. He based it on the **Bard of Armagh**. This had already been changed into **A Handful of Laurel** and this was also a forerunner to **St James Infirmary**, which we shall study in a second book in this series. (Note that **Streets of Laredo** is played in ¾ time like *Down in the Valley*, pages 16 and 17 of this book).